My Passionate Thoughts

A Book of Poetry and thought, motivated by love and personal relationships.

By Rayquan Diamond A.M. Kamau

COPYRIGHT PAGE

My Dedication

I am dedicating this book, to all of the women, in my past and present, who took part in my upbringing and helped, to raise me. I learned something from all of you and it is all appreciated. I love you and thank you.

Table of Contents

Preface

Welcome to the mind of Rayquan Diamond Abdu-Masad Kamau. I truly hope that my little book of poetry is entertaining, as well as, insightful and helpful. My goal is to make you smile, as much, as it is to make you think. The poems I have written were inspired by and for different reasons. Some, of the poems, were inspired by my personal life experiences, while some were inspired by other people's experiences. Some were inspired by random thoughts and others by deep thoughts, that spanned over longer periods of time and experiences. Some are political, some are religious, some are opinionated, some are based on truths, while others are nothing more, than my passionate thoughts.

I set this book up, into a way, that first provides sort of a prelude, or "introduction", to the following poem. The introduction will provide, to you, the ideas, the motivation, thoughts, a breakdown or an explanation, of how the following poem came to be. After the introduction, the poem will follow. You also have the option of going straight to the poem. The poems have been left in the original formats, in which I first typed them. I added the "introductions", in order to provide some extra layers and try to provide an understanding to each particular piece of art, if needed. Some of the introductions also offer, what I believe to be helpful advice, while dealing, with the rest of the world. The introductions may discuss an event that took place, an opinion, a concept, a truth, a theory, my mindset, feelings or, what I would like to believe, my sense of logic.

Some of the thoughts, opinions and ideas you may agree with, others you may not. I would love to discuss my poems with you, if ever given a chance to do so. In the meanwhile, please, find some family and friends, to read and discuss my poems with. Gather around a fire-pit, pour yourself a drink...or "whatever" and let the discussions begin.

The best way to enjoy, my books of poetry, is to keep your mind and imagination wide open. Pour yourself a glass of your favorite beverage, partake in your favorite "method of relaxation", kick back and enjoy.

THANK YOU!!

LOVE

Love, one of the most extreme emotions that anyone can experience, outside of rage, greed, lust, hate and the other extreme emotions, that are also classified as deadly sins, in religious text. Excuse me for going "Star Trek", but extreme emotions, such as "Love", has the ability of ridding most human beings of their ability to rationalize and use logic. Even...during those times where that ability, to do so, can be life changing, or even life threatening. Many, of us, seem to forget that emotions are not governed by logic, reason, rationality, or rules and they affect us all differently, for different reasons. What makes me cry, may make you laugh, what makes you smile, could make me hate and what makes you angry, may have no effect on me, at all, whatsoever. As far as, the effects of emotions go, Love is no different. This makes it very difficult to determine how someone will or should behave, when they are experiencing "Love".

It is amusing, to me, whenever I hear someone try to rationalize someone's behavior, during a relationship, with someone they were in love with. Some of the behavior, that people try to rationalize, is positive behavior and some of it is very negative behavior. Most people don't put a whole lot of attention into the "positive behavior". They simply say "Oh they're in love and that is how people who are in love behave." But, oh, how things change when the behavior becomes negative. All of the self-proclaimed Sigmund Froids and "Life Coaches" begin to breakout their pads, pens and magnifying glasses. They start to apply labels, verdicts and prescriptions. They pass judgment, as to what these people are or are not, were or were not. The worst judgements are when these people proclaim that these individuals were not "truly in love". They believe that how could something, as beautiful as "love", be surrounded by such negativity and turmoil. It doesn't make any rational sense to them. They forget that love is nothing more than an emotion. Love is neither ugly nor beautiful. Love simply becomes whatever it is those two individuals make it. Whatever love becomes, in a relationship, rather that is good or bad, it is still love.

So, be careful when you decide to "console" someone in love and say things like "That is not real love.", "That's infatuation.", "That's puppy love.", "That's lust or obsession.", "How could they truly love you, if this is how they treat you?", "How could you truly love them, if this is how you treat them?", or, my favorite, "How could they possibly love this person, while this person is treating them in such a negative way?". Many people simply do not understand that love has nothing to do with a person's personality or the traits that they have learned, adopted, or have been born with. Whoever they were before they fell in love, will be that same person, after they fall in love. There is no magical pixie, that flies over your head, or that other person's head sprinkling pixie dust, in order to make you both become different people, simply because you are now in love. If he or she was horrible before, then he or she will be horrible after and if he or she was beautiful before, they will continue to be beautiful afterwards.

I am going to share with you a question, I love to use as an example, when I attempt to explain love's effects on relationships. In addition to, how it does and does not effect people's personalities. Here is the question. If you were to fall in love with Jeffrey Dahmer and Jeffrey Dahmer was to fall in love with you, would he stop being Jeffrey Dahmer? The answer is usually and most definitely "No". He will always be Jeffrey Dahmer and now he is in love with you! So, please don't break his heart...for your sake. The response is usually a very chilled laugh, as in "funny, but not funny", but they usually get the point. They learn that love, itself, will not change who a person is. It will not force them to treat you right and it will not force you to treat them right.

Another area of love that people have a hard time understanding is that it is more important to like whom you are with, then it is to love whom you are with. It is very easy to be in love with someone that you don't like. I get this question all the time "How can you love someone that you don't like?" They don't realize how common it is! It happens, all of the time, and you see it everywhere. Right now, as you read this book, there is someone, at home, angry, hurt and crying, because the very person, that they are in love with, has hurt them, often continuously. When you don't like someone, you either don't like how they treat you, don't like what they stand for, don't like how they carry themselves, don't like their method of communication, don't like their habits, and etcetera. If too many of those "dislikes" are true, then guess what? There is very good chance that you don't like them. You may "Love" them, but you don't like them! Most people that are "happily" in love, usually, really like the person, whom they are in love with. They like their conversation, they like what they have in common, they like what they stand for, how they carry themselves and etcetera.

With all that being said, the most important thing, to focus on, in a relationship, is that person and who they are. You want to pay a great deal of attention to your levels of compatibility, how they treat you, how well you communicate with that person, how well you get along and how good do they make you feel mentally, emotionally ....and otherwise. You must understand, that if you spend enough time with anybody, the love will come. However, it does not mean that you will be happy. Simply put.....It is not the love that makes a couple happy. It is who those people are and how they treat each other, that will make them happy. Love is only the bonus and it is only what you make it.

Don't Get Love Twisted

Many of you ask the question...

What is love?

&

I say...

Does it matter.

I mean

should we really waste time,

trying to discover

what makes it tick,

what makes it work,

or

why it exists...

It just does.

Whether you feel it should be or not,

or

whether you want it to or not,

it does not matter.

Because love does not care about...

YOUR OPINION.

How you feel it should be.

How you feel it should act.

How you feel it should treat you.

Love does not care.

So don't expect it to.

Just try your best to enjoy & hold on to the good.

Because, sometimes it will come with the bad.

And

If you want,

build all the walls that you can build,

put up all the protection that

YOU BELIEVE

make you feel safe...

Silly mortal...

Love is not human.

Love is not restricted.

Love is not bounded.

Love can't be held hostage.

Love cannot be controlled.

Love has no rules,

no mercy

&

point Mothafuckin blank

LOVE CANNOT BE STOPPED!

So regardless of what any

self-diluted,

pumped up,

on his or her own game

has told you.

Love cannot be ruled by games & logic.

Because,

To put it plain & simple

Love's a bad mothafucka!

So when it hits your doorstep,

respect it,

learn it,

understand it,

cherish it

&

most importantly,

share it.

But...

!!NEVER!!

try to rule it

or

master it.

Why...

For this reason:

How can an existence with limits,

master an existence without limits?

Think about it.

And,

In the meanwhile,

PLEASE,

Don't get Love twisted.

COMPATIBILITY

Money, beauty, sex, power... are usually the features that will attract one human being to another. I have fallen victim, to this truth, on far too many occasions. Unfortunately, this truth is also responsible, for too many, of the weak, unstable, dysfunctional, shallow and, at times, volatile relationships we witness, on a daily basis. I can not deny that those features are definite bonuses, but they are also very, very far from being the most important aspects, of what I would call a "healthy relationship". Money and power pays the bills and improves a couple's social options. The right sex partner can immensely satisfy those physical urges, that a couple may experience and beauty.....well.....a little "eye candy" never hurts. In addition, beauty and good sex can help keep the passion and desire, in a relationship, at a very high level. I am pretty sure we all either know or have heard of a couple, who's ability, to stay in the relationship, is solely based on the great sex they have with one another. Outside of the bedroom...its Baghdad, Vietnam and the Middle East, all rolled into one toxic relationship. I have had the benefit of experiencing this sort of relationship, first hand. It is not fun and can be very difficult to exit, for both partners. It reminds me of a quote, that I have heard several times, over and over again, on a song, TV show, or from various individuals. "My mind is saying "No" while my body is saying "yes"!" I have a feeling, that this is a quote or situation, we all can relate to.

The only aspect of a relationship, that I have seen hold a relationship together, is the level of "compatibility", between the two individuals, in the relationship. The more compatible the couple is, the stronger the bond or relationship will be. And "Compatibility" doesn't always mean possessing all of the same personality traits. There are some areas of personality that you want to have in common and there are a few areas that you do not want to have in common.

Here are some examples of what I refer to as "compatible likenesses", which, I believe, are very beneficial to the strength of a relationship. The types of entertainment, that each partner enjoys, are very important aspects, for a couple to have in common. It helps to insure that the couple will enjoy their free time together, rather that be at home, in front of a television, on vacation, or while spending a night on the town. When a couple does not enjoy the same types of entertainment, it can and often does create serious problems. It usually leads to less time being spent with one another and preferring to spend their free-time alone, with others, or "another", who enjoy the same forms of entertainment. Sometimes, even if they do force themselves to participate in their mate's preferred forms of entertainment, over-time, the one forcing themselves usually end up resenting the activity or showing serious dissatisfaction or signs of disinterest, for the activity. This, in turn, will upset the significant other, who enjoys the activity, and fuel their resentment for their partner. The raising of children, desired location of residence, type of residence, political and religious beliefs are other examples of personality traits a couple should have in common, in order to help insure the peace and strength in a relationship.

Even, when it comes to communication, having enough in common is important. Both members may be great communicators, but having too many differences, may still lead to conflict and resentment. Or, the lack of having enough, in common, may lead to a partner developing a reasonable motivation, to simply leave the relationship.

In some cases, not having certain personality traits, in common, are an actual benefit to the relationship and are what I refer to as "compatible differences". Here is an example, of possessing common traits, that could result in conflict between two partners. If one member, in the relationship, is an ambitious hard worker, who would love to go home to his partner, who just so happens to be a home-body or "homemaker ", that member would have a serious problem, with a partner, who was just as hardworking and ambitious. That partner, in many cases, would be just as busy and working too hard, in their own career, to be a homemaker, waiting around for their mate to get home.

A couple's likenesses, as well as their differences, need to be compatible likenesses and differences. This next piece illustrates "compatible likenesses".

REWARD

I'm offering a reward, if you're interested, if you're curious…

There is a missing person. It's got me concerned, upset & furious.

Cause I can't seem to find this person and, believe me, I've looked hard & long.

From the highest hilltops, to the lowest valley. I can't figure out what I'm doing wrong.

So please, I need your help. This is fact not fiction.

If you need the details, this is my only description:

She loves long walks in the parks, picnics by the lake.

She loves a good bar-B-Q. She also likes to bake.

She loves a good movie, like she loves good music.

She has a strong intelligence & she isn't scared to use it.

She likes to stay in shape, so she's concerned about her health.

She's not scared to pursue her own dreams, her own business, her own wealth.

She likes nice things. She likes to travel. She likes to dress.

She loves to be close to her man. She loves to be caressed.

She has no problem giving the right man her all.

She will be there to help him stand tall if ever he falls.

If her man is down for her, she will give him her last.

She loves to get up, get out & get something. She's not the kind to sit on her ass.

She loves a good kisser. In the rain, she likes to cuddle.

She loves amusement parks, likes to be carried over a puddle.

She respects a gentleman, just like I respect a lady.

She likes to be held all night by her man, as if she was his baby.

She loves candlelight dinners and she loves knowing me.

She loves live R&B, Blues, Jazz & Poetry.

Wherever she goes, she just likes to have fun.

She loves to take candlelight bubble baths with her man, champagne and a sponge

She loves to be passionate and in the bedroom she's a freak.

She's down to get dirty, likes to be kissed from her head to her feet.

She doesn't hold anything back, when it comes to being kinky, she's a thug.

She's so spontaneous. It don't matter where we make love.

As long as, it's just me & her. Cause, she don't play that sharing shit.

Unless I want a fat lip, endangered dick, pistol whipped, or some tires slit.

Cause, she don't play that. I mean, she can get crazy.

But, as long as, I don't play her, she will never, ever play me.

She cherishes a good man and on everything she will swear.

As long as, I love & respect her, she ain't going nowhere.

So, if you know, or have seen this person, please don't wait,

dial 8 1 6 - 7 2 6 - 3 7 2 8.

This is my compatible soulmate, the one, my future bride-to-be.

And, if you didn't know by now, this woman is just like me.

So, I really need your help. For this woman, I got it bad.

And, as a reward, I will give you every single thing that I have.

Thank You, So Sincerely.

So Many People, Very Few Individuals

There are almost 7 billion people on this big, blue, beautiful marble, that we call "earth", for those of us who speak English. If I had to guess...I would say that only about 70 million are what would qualify as being considered a "true Individual". Now, some of you may be thinking "No two individuals are alike". Well, in all actuality, physically and even mentally, this is true. Although, I am not talking physical, mental traits and experiences. I am specifically talking about social behaviors, traits and habits. Unfortunately, most humans have a strong desire to "fit in" and "do as they do". To a great extent, this desire is understandable, since one of the most governing human want and need is to be accepted. So, unfortunately, this desire leads people to adopt habits, behaviors and mindsets, of the apparent majority. In some cases, this works out and is often a benefit, in those cases. In other cases, it does not work out and the results are, much less than satisfactory, unproductive and, at times, even destructive.

This next poem reflects to how too many men, put far more focus, into appealing to their bros, then they do appealing to the woman, in their lives. They appear to be more concerned about "What will my homies think?", instead of being more concerned about what their wives or girlfriends would think, or how they would feel. Some women even make the mistake of accepting this, as normal male behavior. Some may even expect it and will look at you mysteriously, if you behave outside, of what is considered normal guy behavior. I am speaking from experience, on this one. I was even told, on a few occasions, that my wanting to be in a relationship, was not normal behavior, for a guy, and occasionally even frowned upon, for it. Let's just say, that I have often had a rough, as much as, an enjoyable learning experience while dating.

I have always been considered the individual, at times, a loner, or what many refer to as "different". I have always been this, due to the fact that I have always desired to do what was right, what I felt was best and, most importantly, what it was that I wanted to do. I went through the whole "good guy" phase, off and on, and I have also been the "bad boy". Both "sides of the coin" has its benefits and its set-backs. I discovered that being what most men are not, often ended up more beneficial to me, even if that benefit did not show itself, during the relationship. Sometimes, it got so bad, that I considered remaining a "bad boy". Since, it often appeared that there were more benefits being one. It is, unfortunately, true that women seem to enjoy the company and presence of a bad boy.

It is also, unfortunately, true that many of these relationships usually end up very badly, for the women involved. After, witnessing the pain caused to these women, as a result of these relationships, I decided that I wanted to avoid being someone's horror story. Some of these women, who found themselves in pain, were family members and friends. The others, I only witnessed from a far. So, I decided to actually care about the needs, wants and desires of the women that I dated, even if it didn't always work out to my benefit. In some cases, I simply didn't always have what that woman wanted or needed, mentally, financially, emotionally and, on very rare occasions, physically(Hate to toot my own horn, but "toot-toot".). Even, in those cases, I truly believe that I did my best. I often received praise, recognition and even "rewards", later on, from some of my exes. Redemption is always nice and it helps to know that you were actually doing the right thing. It feels good to know that you were not the typical "bad guy" and that it was not directly or solely your fault. It is always nice to know that you did not become "the negative stereotype", in any situation, and that you left a good impression, of yourself, with that woman, even if it didn't work out. Well...at least, it makes me smile.

Not Any Man

Any man can kiss a woman's lips.

> But, not any man can kiss a woman's thoughts.

Any man can hold a woman in his arms.

> But, not any man can hold on to a woman's dreams and her wishes.

Any man can caress a woman's face.

> But, not any man can caress a woman's inner beauty.

Any man can massage & rub a
    woman's neck, her back & her
    shoulders.

    But, not any man can massage
        & rub away her
        problems....her troubles.

Any man can wipe away a woman's
tears.

    But, not any can wipe away
        herpains, her hurts & her
        sorrows.

        And of course...

Any man can have sex with a
woman's body.

But, it takes a special kind of
man to make love to a
woman's soul.

You see, there are too many men
trying to be any man instead of
trying to be what any man can not
be,

that special kind of a
man........just like me.

Communication in the Bedroom

My first experience with this particular subject, occurred when I was 16. A young lady, by the name of Kyra, that I was crazy about, invited my brother and I to her friend's house, to hang out. Luckily, her friend did not live too far, from my brother and I, so we made a "mad dash" a few blocks to her friend's house. We hung out, talked, joked around, laughed and since the parents were not home, we eventually went to our own little corners.

At this time, I was extremely inexperienced, being that I was only 16 and had, very recently, lost my virginity. So, of course, I fumbled around with the foreplay, for what seemed like forever, waiting for her to give me a sign for the "go-ahead". It never happened. So, eventually, I made a fatal mistake. I built up the courage, in order, to ask, respectfully......if it was Ok to have sex! Immediately, it turned the heated, hot and sexy moment into an awkward and clumsy one and her reply became a hesitant and disappointing "no". So, we attempted to play off the "moment of rejection" and finish off the night.

Once, my brother and I arrived back to the house, I received a call from Kyra and our conversation eventually led into the "moment of rejection". It was brought to my attention, for the first time, but definitely not the last time, that most women expects for a man to "sense" the moment and make a move. This concept took a very, very, very long time for me to understand and master..... Who am I kidding?! I haven't mastered a damn thing! Unfortunately, It is still, til' this very day, like "rolling the dice" or "spinning the wheel". Sometimes you hit your point and sometimes you roll a "crap". Even through my experiences, in marriage, I am left having to guess if she is in the mood....or not?! Does she want me to be extra freaky....or not!? Does she want me to get to the point and make it quick....or not?! Is she saying that she doesn't want to have sex, or does she want me to work a little harder to get her in the mood....or not? The list goes on and on.

I have had moments where the women were mad that I did not try, as well as, moments where they were mad that I did try. I have had moments were the ladies were disappointed that I didn't treat them like 2 dollar whores, off the strip. In addition, to experiencing moments, with a significant other, where our sexual escapades were usually, if not always, "Buckwild". But, on one particular day, she would suddenly want a more gentle and passionate touch, without informing me, of the menu change. It is a serious mood destroyer to hear your intimate partner scream out, in the middle of having sex, "Why are you just fucking me?!!". That outburst came, complete, with tears. You should have seen the, almost terrifying, look of confusion on my face. I had no clue as to what just happened. Luckily.....I guess....she then curled up, into my arms, slightly sobbing, eventually falling asleep and soon I followed. When we awoke the next day, she apologized and explained to me that, on top of having a bad day, she began to "flashback", during our sexual moment, to a prior bad relationship, which resulted into her emotional outburst. She then explained to me that, on that particular night, she needed to be made love too, but, unfortunately, I didn't get the memo.

Look, I understand being in the moment and then attempting to, naturally, react to that moment, but sometimes it tremendously helps to know, exactly, how your partner wants to be loved and be made love too. Especially, when your mood is outside, of the usual.

Let it be known
(Make Love or be Fucked)

Damn you so sexy, I can't believe you all mine.

From your lips to your fingertips, divine and just too fine.

Let me carry you through this door baby, lay you down on our bed.

Let me take off your shoes, as I place a kiss gently, on top your forehead.

As I begin slowly taking off your stockings, you begin biting that bottom lip.

Slowly moving them thick hips, rubbin' this dick. Shit, you a trip!

And, you know it. If you are down, I'm ready. All I need to hear is two words.

Make love or be fucked? How do you want it served?

Strawberry romance, cherry passion, slow grinded whip cream, on a silver platter.

Or, a down & dirty thrust, with a monster bust, hard bangin' makin' yo' teeth clatter.

Just let it be known. Because, I do care about how you feel and how I make you feel.

I don't ever want you to feel like a hoe. You must always know, our love is real.

So, come and give me a tender hug, if you want some of this love.

Or, you can bounce that ass and grab this dick, if you want some of this thug.

Or, do you want me to kiss every single every single inch, of your luscious, tasty, knees, toes and elbows.

Slowly lick then flip that clit, between my lips. Until, you scream "Stop, oh, you can't take it no mo'!".

Or, do you want me to grab them ankles and make a wish, lick that clit, like a dog with no dish.

Hold yo' ass down like a brotha' so pissed and I won't let go, til' I hear you scream "Shit!".

Just let it be known. Baby, choose your song.

Cause, I can either do that ass so right, or I can do that ass so wrong.

So, do you wanna' brotha' who's soft and tender or do you wanna' nigga' gone wild.

I can make you feel like a queen in bed, or I can treat you like a mothafuckin' stepchild.

How do you want it?! Cause this Hennessee's talkin' crazy!

Baby beau, I'm yo' blunt! I don't care how you blaze me!!

But, I do care about how I blaze you. So, just let it be known.

You are the Queen of our castle, ruler of my world, mother of my home.

So, don't worry about if I care. Forget all that strife!

Whether we fuck or make love, you will always be my wife!

Goodness! I see you're shakin' that ass. You must want it like that!

You want some of this gangsta'! Time to blow out that back!

You better find shelter, cause I'm bringin' down the thunder!

You will feel this seventh wonder! A voodoo spell I am about to put you under!

But, before we get started. Before, we do what we do.

I must let you know... I will always love you.

Some people are simply not worth the time and energy!!

One day, I was on the phone, with a little cutie I had met, while I was out enjoying myself. The conversation started out as usual, with the common introductory conversation fillers. Of course, it began with Introducing myself, who I am, what I do, what I am into. She then introduces herself, who she is, what she does and what she is into. We talked about our jobs, what our hobbies were, our zodiac signs, kids or no kids, favorite types of music, what we like to do for fun and how long has it been since our last relationships. This last line of questioning morphed into something I had not planned for. Usually, in the beginning of a relationship, or when simply getting to know someone, this question is given a short and sweet response. Which, normally, consists of the amount of time the relationship lasted and a very brief description, of why it ended. Most people do not want to expose too much of their business, or personal life, too soon.

But, not this time...she began to pour it all out. After, around 45 minutes to an hour, she described, in full detail, all of the ins and outs of her relationship, with this particular brotha'. By this time, I knew that any plans, that I once had, were nothing more than a fabulous dream...or a really good XXX movie. What I have, now, is a temporary job, as a personal therapist. So, I made myself comfortable, grabbed my glasses, my pen and a notebook and continued to listen. I did my best to provide as much advice and personal therapy, as I could, according to my ability. It was very obvious that this relationship was still fresh, if not still ongoing. She truly loved this guy and she, most definitely, was not the one in control. She was in one of those unbalanced relationships where she was the only full-time member in the relationship and he was more like an Uber driver. He participated in the mutual benefits, whenever it was convenient for him to do so and he most definitely enjoyed the "rides", when he needed a "pick me up". Not only was he a Part Time Lover, whenever he decided to be in her presence, it was like living with a rabid pit-bull. I don't recall her ever saying that he abused her physically, but he definitely abused her mentally and emotionally. It seemed, as if, no matter what she would try to do or try not to do, it was still never good enough. He would bark, yell, complain and throw out insults, as if it entertained him. It sounded, as if, it made him feel good to do so.

After, about another an hour, of listening, and trying to give her best advice I could give her, she decided that she was going to give him a call. In her plan, she stated that when she does call him, she was going to be as nice, polite and loving, as she could possibly be. She said that it did not matter how belligerent or disrespectful he would be to her. Regardless, of his behavior, she would not allow him, to get under her skin. Her plan was to become MLK, Ghandi, or someone else who believed in peaceful protest and "Kill'em with kindness". I listened to about another 20 minutes of her horrible, but good intentioned, plan and became slightly irritated. She honestly believed that this asshole would stop being an asshole, as long as she continued to be as nice as she had already been this whole time. So, I informed her, of the great possibility, that most people simply are who they are. I truly believe most people do not change. They may improve in certain areas, but they do not change. There is no way, in hell, she should continue being nice too and dealing with someone, who is treating her like shit! I then explained to her, that if he continues acting like an asshole, treat him like an asshole, fuck him!

After, making that final suggestion, to the troubled sister, my eyes lit up! I, temporarily, forgot all about this woman's problems and had come to realize what my next poem would be about. Once, I was able to dismiss myself, from the conversation, I immediately began writing the poem that I am now about to share with you.

Fuck'em

Do you know a dude, who's attitude's rude,

personality is crude, just straight rotten like
spoiled

food?

If they act like dicks, then treat'em like dicks...

Fuck'em!

If you know a chic who's attitude is bunk. She
pulls

scandalous stunts,

using the junk in her trunk.

If they act like cunts, then treat'em like cunts...

Fuck'em!

If you know a Joe, who's woman loves to give
private

shows. His anger grows.

Cause, she blows many men and much mo.

If they act like hoes, then treat'em like hoes...

Fuck'em!

If you know a girl or guy, who likes to make people

cry.

Even though they try and have no real good reason

why.

If they act like assholes, then treat'em like assholes...

Fuck'em!

If you know a fellow, with no courage straight yellow.

When he sees trouble, his legs turn to peach jello.

If they act like pussies, then treat'em like pussies...

Fuck'em!

Do you know a girl who will rock anybody's world?

Or, a guy who will pay anybody to make his toes curl?

If they act like tricks, then treat'em like tricks...

Fuck'em!

If you are currently nursin', someone who keeps you cursin'.

Their brain is in reversion, just a stupid ass person.

If they act like dildos, then treat'em like dildos...

Fuck'em!

If you know anyone, who knows anyone.

Whom don't like this poem, don't think it's much fun.

I'll pull out my finger. Yeah, you know which one

and

Fuck'em!

Money without someone to share it with

Imagine you won the lottery. You cash in the ticket, take care of your family, buy a beautiful home, on several acres, complete with a pool and rec-house. You purchase a collection of the nicest vehicles you could imagine, including a yacht and private jet. You invest into a few business ventures, in order to hold on to your new found wealth. You smile...so far, you have made all of the right moves. You're feeling very proud and very content. As a reward, to yourself, you begin taking expensive trips.

At first, your trips are local. You know... the usual "go-to" destinations, such as Disney World, Disney Land, LA and Hollywood. You spend a month in Vegas, then a month in New York, followed by New Jersey, Chi-town, The "Power & Light District" in KC, Florida, Washington DC, Dallas, Houston, Atlanta, New Orleans and of course Hawaii. Then your trips become more eccentric, foreign and exotic. You begin to travel to places like Jamaica, Rio De Janeiro, Brazil, Puerto Rico, the Virgin Islands, London, Paris, Switzerland, Italy, Greece, China, Japan, South Africa, the Ivory Coast and Egypt. You even take the time out to organize a trip to see the "Aurora Lights" in Alaska. While observing the lights, in some of the most finest amenities, Alaska has to offer, you realize that you have no one there experiencing these moments with you.

There is no one sitting beside you, to discuss the wonders of the multi-colored spectrum of lights in the sky. No one to help you google how the lights are formed, while you sip on your favorites beverages. No one to sit beside you, while enjoying the warmth coming from the beautiful fireplace. No one to observe the pyramids with, no one to harass the Buckingham Palace guards with, no one to smoke a "doobie" with in Switzerland, no one to lay on the beach with...there is no one. It is just you, your blanket, the fire and the remote. You're alone. You get on your private plane to travel home alone. At the airport, you step into your limousine alone, just to travel back to your large, beautiful, quiet house...alone.

There is a long history of wealthy, or rich, men and women, who became depressed and in some cases even suicidal, after discovering how simply having a lot of money is not enough, to be happy. From, what I have observed. After, you have taken care of all of your personal needs and wants, money only creates genuine happiness, when you are able to use it to bring happiness to and take care of the people, or person, you love and care about the most. When you can bring smiles to their faces. When your immediate circle can participate in the experiences of enjoying your spoils. Maybe it's just me, but I do not see the benefit of waving a victory flag, to an empty field. I pray that, if you ever obtain wealth and riches, you also have or find a true love to share it with.

Money - Love = Nothing

2004 Bentley, no one to ride with.

Jamaican sunsets, no one to see it with.

First Class airline trips, no one to fly with.

Money - Love = Nothing

10,000 dollar credit cards, no one to shop with.

Costa Rican shores, no one to dive with.

Moet and Christyle, no one to pop with.

Money - Love = Nothing

Las Vegas Casinos, No one to loose with.

Great escapes to Hawaii, and no one to hide with.

300 foot Yacht, No one to cruise with.

Money - Love = Nothing

300 dollar Lobster dinners, no one to eat with.

8000 dollar King size canopy waterbed, no one to sleep with.

Half a million dollar home, no one to share it with.

They say with money comes trouble, no one to bare it with.

10 fancy cars, No one to lend them to.

100,000 dollar ring, no one to give it to.

20 dozen roses, No one to hand them to.

200,000 dollar wedding, no one to say I do.

Life can be an exciting trip, but I have no one to ride with.

My life has gone by, with all this money & I have no one to die with.

Money – Love = Nothing

CONFUSED

I have often heard women describe the "man of their dreams". Usually, they begin with the physical description. You know….the most common traits of being handsome, or a "pretty boy", with muscular details. Next, they follow up with more personal taste, such as, eye color, hair color, dark skinned, light skinned, hair length, tall, short, beard, no beard, heavy, thin and style of dress. The description then becomes real personal, filled with dreams, desire and emotion. This is where the confusion begins. Much like the most common desired physical traits, the personality traits also have a common group, which are hardworking, kind, romantic, a gentleman, a good conversationalist, a good listener, good father, not abusive, loyal and, most importantly, faithful. Which are all great qualities, for a husband to be.

Unfortunately, a few months, to a few years later, I will either run into these same women, or actually encounter them on a regular basis. For many of them, the men that they either date, accept, settle down with or, in some cases, marry, do not fit the original description of their "dream guy". It appears that there are women who, often, become attracted to the opposite version of the guy, that would better suit them and lead to a healthier relationship. This behavior is, unfortunately, very common and can be compared to having a bad habit. A habit that you enjoy, find difficult to "kick" and is very bad for your health. In many of those cases, the bad habit is socially known, as a woman being in love with a "bad boy".

It has even reached the point where many men believe that the "bad boy" image will give them a better chance at meeting and dating women. To make it worst, there is plenty of evidence, all around us, supporting this belief. Unfortunately, there is a large number of women whose behavior, along with their significant other choices, will make men, often, think twice about the whole "nice guy" routine. Some women actually view good guys, as "push-overs". Even I refuse to allow myself to go back to the man I once was, simply because the man I am now gets better results. I actually have a fear of behaving too much like a "nice guy". I now have a genuine fear of experiencing, what I have already experienced, from the women, in my past, whom I believe I was being too nice to.

I will never want to be an absolute bad experience for a woman, but I definitely keep it interesting and not always in a "good guy" kind of a way. Maybe, it works because certain women require a little excitement, they love a challenge and it cures boredom...I don't know. What I do know is, if these women really want to be treated with true respect and have men who meet higher quality expectations, they need to reject and avoid the men, who do not measure up to these expectations. In the meanwhile, here is my next piece of written art.

You Say You Want This

I've got somethin' to say, because I'm a little ticked.

Some ladies have done lost it! Mentally, ya'll straight sick.

Now, I'm a tell it like it is. I hope you ain't scared of the truth.

Cause I'm about to hit a home run, like my name was Babe Ruth.

Hold on give me a minute, cause I'm about to get up in it.

See I'm mad. Yawl done did it. So, I have no choice but to get with it.

So pull up a chair. So, you & I can have a chat.

Since you say you want this, but you keep runnin' to that.

Since I was a little boy, my elders told me "To a woman be kind.".

Now that I'm grown...them fools done lost they mind!

Cause I've tried everything. Please, let me explain.

When this is all through, you will see I'm not insane.

You see, I've wined & I've dined, dressed & caressed.

I've opened doors & much more. Now, I'm stuck with this "S" on my chest.

If you don't understand now, you will by the end of this chat.

<u>Since you say you want this, but you keep runnin' to that.</u>

I mean, you say you want a man, who will guarantee all your needs.

But, you still with that same man, who is guaranteed to make your lip bleed.

And, didn't you say you want a man who will hold you all night?

Then you need to get rid of that one, who barely comes home... alright.

Didn't you tell me, that you wanted a man who will always be true?

Why you still in love that man, who does your friend, before he comes home to do you?

Don't act like you don't know, you told me about those scratches on his back!

<u>Since you say you want this, but you keep runnin' to that.</u>

I keep hearing sad stories about how the past years have been so rough.

But, in seconds, you run back, you must like it, you can't get enough.

You say you want a good man, but you keep wanting that dog.

Your actions back up everything I'm sayin'. If they don't then, I'm a bullfrog.

Since, I don't croak, it's no joke! You know I ain't lyin'.

I am always trying to make you smile. But, you still in love with that one who keeps you cryin'.

You can frown all you want. I'm tellin' nothin' but facts!

<u>Since you say you want this, but you keep runnin' to that.</u>

Didn't you say you wanna man who could hold down a job.

Then why your man in jail for selling drugs and trying to rob.

46

After, he spent five years in the joint, you kicked out your new man.

You waited all this time for him to come home, but he moves in with another woman.

Now you upset, talkin' about seeking revenge.

But, ain't you the one who said you wanted a challenge.

Someone who's rude, with attitude in his pack.

See you couldn't want this, when you keep runnin to that.

So ladies, mean what you say and mean what you want.

Cause, when I see that shit happen, I laugh & I taunt.

Because, season after season, I keep pleadin' & pleasin'.

No matter, how good I am and for no apparent reason.

I lose a good girl, to a good for nothin' Joe.

He gets labeled a G, a player, and I get labeled a Captain Save-a-hoe.

If that's what you are, then I guess that's wrap.

I want to give you this, but in order to even have you, I have to be that.

SORRY......

My Dirty Mind

My brother and I used to share constant laughs and entertain ourselves, by observing, waiting and looking, for the next opportunity, to find obscene, freaky, sexual references and comparisons, in the world around us. Yes, my brother and I were the living versions of "Beavis and Butthead". No person or situation was safe from our relentless search for a good laugh, based on a sexual or perverted insinuation. Billboards, signs, comments, titles, statements, speeches, literature, acts, actions, behavior, statues, various types of artwork, movies, conversations, or anything in our presence would fall victim to our explicit comedic imaginations.

We would also play a little "inside game" with friends and family. Where we would have a general conversation with an unknowing participant, while speaking in sexual or perverted "code". The participant would believe they were having a normal conversation, not knowing they were actually part of an explicit dialogue. Usually, while one of us was engaging the victim, the other would retreat to a corner, due to uncontrollable laughter. The goal was to talk sexual, without using any obvious or common sexual words, phrases, or language. This goal is not always easy to accomplish, but for two bored male teenagers, it was nothing short of abundant, carnal fun and laughter. This next poem is my attempt, at playing this dirty little mind game.

The Spiciest Pickle at the Candy Store

Welcome...

To my forever lasting candy store...

With your permission, please, forget the competition,

I am guaranteed to have more.

What can I do,

For someone like you today?

Can I get you something sweet,

Maybe a Chocolatey treat.

Before, you go out & play.

No...

Oh, you don't want it sweet.

You want it on fire.

Only, something strong, lasting all night long,

Will satisfy your desire.

Umh, I see...

Do you want me to place this goodie,

In your back...pack I mean.

I have, exactly, what you are asking.

Guaranteed to make you scream.

Yeah, I see you smiling.

I knew this is what you want.

It's real, real nice, with a very low price,

And your dreams it will pleasantly haunt.

We have various dips and sprinkles,

to go along with this treat.

Wipes, towels and napkins,

to keep your hands, body and face neat.

It, only, comes in one serving size.

So, I hope you brought an appetite.

I keep it hear, on the middle shelf.

I keep the area very clean and the lid real tight.

Please, help me pull it off...

Sometimes, I have to give it a jiggle,

cause it can get fickle.

After, all that strokin', gropin'& pokin', we finally got it open.

Here, pull out a pickle.

Well...

It looks, as if, it's the only one
we have...

Then, again, it's the only one
you'll need.

This will be one taste you can't
erase.

So, please try & watch the
greed.

Cause, too much will bring
tears to yo' eyes

and too little just won't do.

It'll make you holla, for that
glass of water,

once this pickle is through.

I mean, forget what you heard.

This, here, is the seventh wonder.

It will make your head spin, frown & then grin,

When you feel this thunder.

And...

When you crave another taste, don't worry I got more.

Forget those other brothers, there is no other.

This here is the spiciest pickle, at the candy store.

So, go ahead try it.

Cause, I can tell that you're excited.

And, If you begin to lose your cool,

Crying, don't know what to do,

Relax... don't fight it.

> Do whatever you want,
>
> Just don't bite it.

Why Your Truth No Longer Matters

Unfortunately, people abuse the trust of others. I am pretty sure that this has been a problem, between human beings, ever since we were blessed with intelligence and free will. Some of us will do and have done great things, with our intelligence and freedoms. While others are inspired or motivated to cause problems, pain and frustration with these gifts. Our ability to use our intelligence and free will, to communicate, is one of those areas, where some of us our able to accomplish great things, while others destroy and create turmoil.

Many women have fallen prey to men, who intentionally mislead these women into believing they are full of good intentions. These men carry out this behavior, in order to abuse and take advantage of the trust offered by these women. There are elders who actually give younger men this advice. "The best way, to get into a woman's heart, is to tell her whatever she wants to hear." Unfortunately, women, actually, do put a lot of attention and focus into what a man has to say and for understandable reasons. Although, there is a weakness, in placing too much focus into what a man has to say. Especially, when you are dealing with a man, whom was blessed with the "Gift of Gab". The "Gift of Gab" is basically having thee exceptional ability to convince, inspire, motivate and manipulate those who listen to you.

So, if woman meets a man, who possesses this ability, he will stand an increased chance of convincing that woman to believe or, at least, consider his intentions. The more gifted he is the stronger the convincing will be. The worst part is I have witnessed and have learned that it really doesn't matter who the man actually is, good or bad. If he can say it right, he will play her right.

Over time, if a woman hears too much of the same lies and nonsense, it becomes too hard to differentiate between the men who are genuine and the ones who have negative intentions. The truth is simply this. What a woman wants to hear is exactly what a woman wants to hear. Those individuals with "The Gift" know this and keeps a list of these desired wants handy, at all times. So, after a while, it all begins to sound the same. It doesn't matter if the guy is true and honest. It becomes hard to tell the difference between a good man telling the truth and a deceptive man telling lies. So, a good hearted and genuine man will get passed over, simply because his skills of delivering his message was not as good as the deceptive guy's delivery. A "Good Guy" does not possess a desire to deceive, due to his nature, but a deceptive guy has the desire, intent and purpose to deceive, in order to gain. So, this purpose motivates them to practice, practice, practice and as the saying goes "Practice makes Perfect".

Usually, either a good guy's intentions sound too good to be true, or it sounds like the same bull they heard 10 times in the past 2 weeks. I have experienced this dilemma on a few occasions. I have met women, in my life, whom I would have seriously worked my hardest, to be everything they have ever dreamed of. But, when I attempted to share my plans and honest intentions, with these women, the plans were dismissed for either sounding too good or because of understandable skepticism. After a few more failures and a whole lot of reflection, I had come to realize I simply needed to get better, at saying what I needed to say. As the saying goes "If you can't impress them with your truth and intelligence, then dazzle them with your bullshit!". The only thing that makes the "Gift of Gab" good or bad are the intentions, of the person using the gift.

My advice to women are simply this. Yes, listen to what he has to say, but after you finish listening, put in the time necessary to truly get to know him and attentively watch him. Make sure his actions back up everything he had to say, and do this over an extended period of time. I'm talking years, not months, just to make sure. Oh, and don't be mistaken, many women possess the "Gift of Gab", as well. So, men too need to be careful and pay more attention to her actions, after they have already heard her words. To put it plain and simple...due to constant abuse and misuse, words are no longer sufficient enough, to know a person's true intentions.

Words of No Use

Ain't this a bitch, another Friday night,

So much beauty, but no true romance in sight.

So here I am just holding up the wall.

Listening to the DJ make his next song call.

Lookin' at the same ol' women, eating the same old grub.

Thinkin' to myself, how you gonna' find a good woman at the club?

I look at all these macks as a thought runs through my dome.

Half the brothas' in here already got good women at home.

And, they're still out here lookin'. Man it's a trip.

I'd trade places with them in a second. They can have this shit.

As, I take another bite into a buffalo wing,

An angel walks in. I thought I heard the heavens sing.

She was as beautiful as true love, skin as soft as a whisper.

I wish I was the doorman right now! Cause, I would love to frisk her!

Time to get it together, move quick and straighten up that back.

But, hold up, I got'ta big problem, I, nowhere near, know how to mack.

You see I take love serious. So, my true heart is the one to blame.

Women like to listen to what a man has to say. I never learned how to play that game.

And I don't like playin. So, I guess my truth is a bore. It straight gets ignored!

I'm still sittin' on the bench, while other brothas' hit high scores.

But, I can't let that stop me. Hell, I got to try.

I cannot let something, so beautiful, simply, pass me by.

So here I go, time to do my thing.

As, I wipe off the sauce, from those buffalo wings.

I begin to step closer. My mind starts thinking.

What should I say to her and, um, is my breath stinking?

I could tell her she's beautiful and damn how fine.

But, I'm pretty sure she hears that shit, all the damn time.

So, what can I say that will help me pull?

I'll take care of all your needs? And, I will, but she's already heard enough of that bull.

What could I say, to separate me from the rest?

Show her I'm the best man, recognize the S on my chest.

But, there is no way that I can show her, in less than 5 minutes.

Because, as far as she believes, I'm just tryin' to get up in it.

Since, most of the men that approach, is full of that trash.

They say they want a piece of her heart, when all they really want, is a piece of that ass.

I could tell her that, if I was GOD, I would give her the world.

That I'm a damn good man, just lookin' for a damn good girl.

Look no further, your king is here.

You don't have to cry no more. I will erase your fears.

No, love is greater. No, heart is bigger.

But, let's keep it real. She heard that from the last nigga.

I don't wanna sound desperate, but I'll eat through them drawls.

I will lick through them jeans and I will bite through that bra.

But, then I'll sound like the rest of them fools.

Fuck it, I'm stuck. I don't know what to do.

So, now I'm up in her face. I want her to stay.

But, what could I do, to make her wanna come my way?

I don't know what to say. My words are of no use.

Thanks, to all these years of unnecessary abuse.

Look, I don't wanna mack, or sound stupid, no bloops and no blunders.

Baby, I just wanna keep it real simple. May, I please just have your number.

Thank you.

Expect What You Give

"Do unto others as you want them to do unto you."....a classic. I believe that it is the fundamental rule of appropriate social behavior. It is the major guiding principal in my life, when it comes to how I interact with people, family, friends, the women I date, associates, business associates and so on. I believe that if everyone in the world, simultaneously, made an honest effort to follow this most basic of principles, at the very least, fifty percent of the world's problems would be solved. War, racism, hunger, unnecessary violence, homelessness, crooked business practices, and all other forms of unfair treatment would disappear. This would cut the world's experience of pain, sadness, frustration and anger in half, if not more. Life would significantly become more reasonable.

The premise or idea behind this "golden rule" is simple. If you would not like the experience of being subjected to an action that you are about to commit, then there is a very good chance that most others would not like it as well. This idea is very true, in most cases. I mean...there is a very small percentage, of the population, who "get a rise" out of receiving abuse. For those individuals, I honestly don't know, don't have a comment, nor a solution. As far as the rest of us are concerned, we hate unfair, unjust and unnecessary pain, conflict and complications just like anyone else. A vast majority of the worlds pain and suffering is caused by someone else's actions, rather those actions are political, personal, or professional, or, at times, even religious.

I personally feel that one of the worst people, on the planet, you could be in a relationship with, is one who has one of these mindsets: "You are not allowed to do what I do.", "It is different when I do it." And "Yes, I know that I did it to you, but what gives you the right to do it to me!". In addition to, those who find excuses and explanations, as to why it is ok for them to commit actions against their partner, while knowing they would not like it being done to themselves. These types of people will commit hurtful acts against someone and then expect for those acts to be accepted or forgiven. Although, if you ever commit one of these very same acts against them, then all hell breaks loose and you become the very essence of evil, in it's human form. "How could you dare?!!"

Yes, I repeat, these individuals are the absolute worst people to be in a relationship with. So, to my beloved human family it is very simple. If you don't like the way it feels, then neither will I (or someone else).

Don't Want It, Don't Give It

I truly don't understand why you're angry, frustrated or mad.

I thought you'd be cool, content, even glad.

I just figured that how you behaved is how you want me to behave.

You only give what you want, a fair is a fair trade.

You got my back, I got yours, or that's how it should be.

I would be there, if I knew you would be there. That's how it would be.

But instead you flaked, so frosted I became.

You established the rules. I just played the game.

And don't be upset, that I am just as good, of a gamer.

You see, I learn from the best and you're a very good trainer.

I love how you show me one thing, switch up, and do another.

So, I tried the move on you and you wasn't happy with this brotha'.

You said that I cheated. My actions were not legal.

Look, honor is my land and truth is my people.

So, I pulled out your playbook, page 22, chapter 8.

I followed your regulations with precision. There can be no debate.

I only did to you, exactly what you did to me.

I don't believe in "tit for tat". "Tat for tat" sounds more like me.

So, if you don't like it, please don't assume that I will.

Please, assume that I do think and, please, assume that I do feel.

The same way you would feel, while being treated in such a way.

How could you think that it's okay, when you don't think that it's okay.

I hope I didn't lose you. Cause, you about to lose me.

It's okay that you chose yourself. Cause, I'm about to choose me.

If you don't want to be alone, don't make me feel alone.

If you don't want me to be a dog, give me more than a bone.

I can only give back, what is given to me, to give.

I can only live out, what is given to me, to live.

When you fall short, you can't have high expectations.

When you're motivated, to complete motivating acts, it increases my motivation.

To do unto them, as they to do unto you...I live it.

So, if you don't want it, please, don't give it.

About the Author

Rayquan Diamond Abdu-Masad Kamau

Was born and raised in Kansas City, Missouri. (He was actually born, at the KU Medical Center, which is, literally, located on the State line. This, actually, makes him Kansas born, if you want to be technical about it! Moving on...) Rayquan has always been in love with the arts. He is a songwriter, rapper and a producer, whom also sketches, sculpts and paints. He proudly refers to himself as being an "Urban Geek" or a "Street Nerd". Because, aside from his "street" upbringing, he also loves the sciences, mathematics, physics, chemistry, astronomy, psychology and all things tech. He has watched every single "Star Wars" series, except the entire original series, and has enjoyed every movie. His fantasy, as a child, was to grow up and become a scientist, as well as, an inventor.

He has spent most of his adult life, as a bail bondsman. Recently, he renewed his license, as a Real Estate Agent and has vowed to, eventually, become a successful Real Estate Investor. Rayquan was born with several, what he refers to, as "GOD Given" gifts and talents. So, in addition, to his "Real Estate" vow he also made a promise, to himself, to share as much of his artistic talent with the world as possible. Before, it is time for him to leave this beautiful world, that GOD has blessed us with. (He loves to and has requested that we capitalize all three letters in the word GOD, when he refers to GOD, or maybe you noticed. Moving on...) He truly hopes that you have enjoyed the poetry in this book and, most importantly, he hopes that he was able to inspire a thought and make you reflect, in one way or another.

You are tremendously appreciated.

Thank You,

Rayquan Diamond Abdu-Masad Kamau

Coming Soon:

"My Extra 2 Cents" A book of poetry inspired by GOD, religion, social topics and politics.
By Rayquan Diamond A.M. Kamau

www.ingramcontent.com/pod-product-compliance
Lightning Source LLC
Chambersburg PA
CBHW060519280326
41933CB00014B/3025